# WARNING

# This book is especially for:

- People who, like myself, passionately love **collaboration**, yet consistently botch it up.

- People who enthusiastically read **self-help books**, yet have trouble finishing them.

- People who strongly believe in the power of **self-awareness**, yet forget to use it.

# TABLE
# OF
# CONTENTS

PREFACE

INSPIRATION

THE DILEMMA: WHEN COLLEAGUES DISCONNECT

AT THE MERCY OR AT THE SOURCE?

HOT HOT HOT BUTTONS

THE CANDY STORY

THE EGO-CLOCK

TWELVE STEPS TOWARD FREEDOM

THE RESOLUTION: WHEN COLLEAGUES RECONNECT

ACKNOWLEDGEMENTS

GLOSSARY

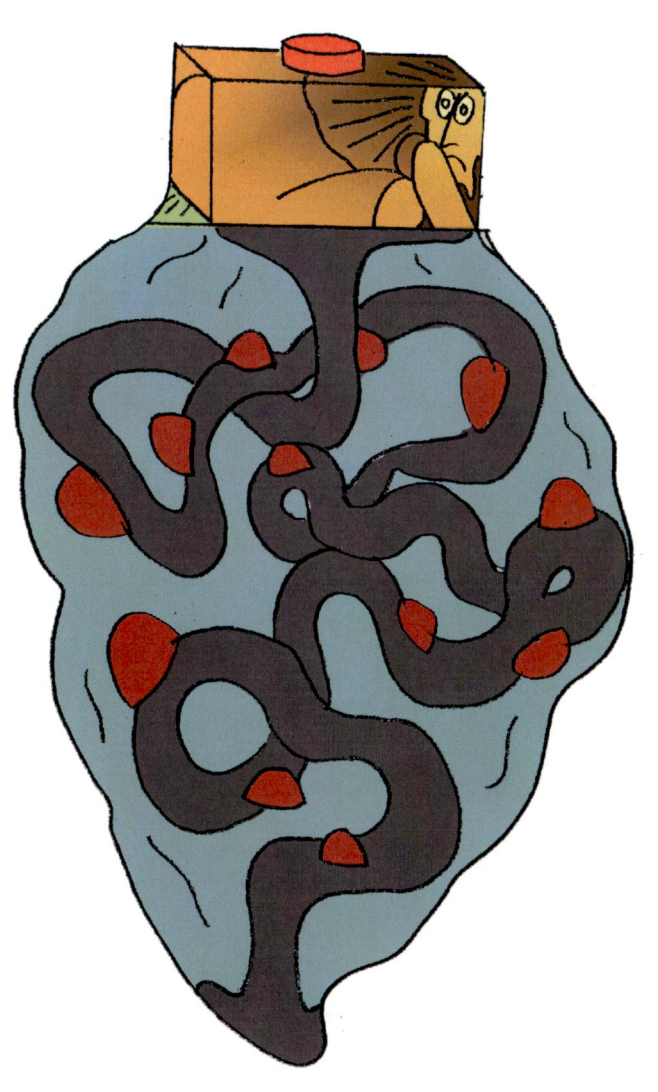

# PREFACE

I wouldn't have been able to fulfill my calling as an artist, if I hadn't first embraced the journey of self-awareness.

As a child, I didn't think I was talented enough to become an artist, so **I stopped drawing**.

But as an adult, consultant, facilitator and executive coach, I overcame my self-limiting beliefs and returned to my **passion** for illustration and storytelling.

This book is the fruit of my transformation and the integration of two passions: **creative expression** and **self-discovery**.

At first, I wanted to write a book about collaboration on my own, involve others as little as possible, not ask for help or feedback. But I had to face the truth that to write about collaboration, I needed to collaborate.

Over the last twenty years, I've been part of *Learning as Leadership* (LAL), a cutting-edge leadership training company that teaches leaders to create sustainable organizations through personal mastery. It's been an extraordinary journey of collaboration, filled with remarkable accomplishments and significant learning bumps.

This book doesn't address all the complexities of working with others. I chose the angle of reflection that I knew best: **how the ego's hot buttons\* get in the way of collaboration and how to break free.**

I believe that since life is inevitably bumpy, learning to overcome our hot buttons is key in creating constructive relationships at work, at home and in our communities. As fallible as I am, I'm wholeheartedly committed to this process!

I hope this book will ignite self-reflections and authentic conversations, provide levity, and inspire rich emotional connections.

# Enjoy!

*\*In this book, the ego refers to a constant preoccupation with one's self-worth.*
*\*\*A hot button is a point of sensitivity that the ego recognizes as a threat.*

**INSPIRATION**

M any of the ideas and concepts in this book are derived from the *Learning as Leadership* methodology (see the glossary). LAL has provided me with a unique framework in which to learn about myself and others, to grow, study, teach, consult, facilitate, rebel and reconcile.

I want to thank my team for allowing me to freely use our invaluable material in creating this book.

You can learn more about Learning as Leadership's story and principles at:

**www.learnaslead.com**

I also want to thank the Arbinger Institute, which has allowed me to use their copyrighted concepts of **"being in the box"** and **"being outside of the box."**

Read more about their leadership principles at:

# www.arbinger.com.

*Layout and publication design completed by* **MAYDAY***: mayday-mayday-mayday.com*

# chapter 1

# The Dilemma: When Colleagues Disconnect

# My team is a fantastic team!

Together we have helped **thousands** of people to become better leaders. By supporting each other to evolve while protecting our core values, we have created miracles and survived disasters. Frankly, we are the most successful collaborative team I know and often, I have the image of us as a group of **joyful musicians** playing a symphony together!

**Except last Friday,** when my colleague Andrea approached me at the coffee machine to share some exciting news.

Like me, Andrea is an executive coach at our leadership company. She has also been studying for an MBA in Sustainability. It is her final year and she needs to define a business project.

# Her words boomeranged in my brain.

Of course, I didn't say any of this because I know it's pathetic to be territorial. However, I couldn't stop my mind chatter: **"She is unrealistic," "She wants to steal my place," "She wants to take over."**

Instead, since I'm a **mature** person with loads of personal mastery training, I asked objective questions to help her think about her business model.

# I imagine that my colleague felt deflated and sad.

As for me, I felt relieved because the "danger" had passed. Yet, I felt ashamed because I was behaving defensively instead of collaboratively.

# Instead of playing music with **Andrea...**

I was in a box, playing an old tape.

# She was probably in a box too.

**B**ut, the truth is that I didn't want to step out of my box, because I didn't want to share my toys. I mean, **my job.**

# chapter 2

# At the Mercy or At the Source?

Like most people, I have my trigger points. When I hit them, I retract into "box mode," a deluded state of confusion driven by fear. I am at the mercy of others and external circumstances.

**B**ut I'm not always in my box. I often reside **at the source**, a state of clarity where I'm a fallible human being with an open heart and a big appetite for life.

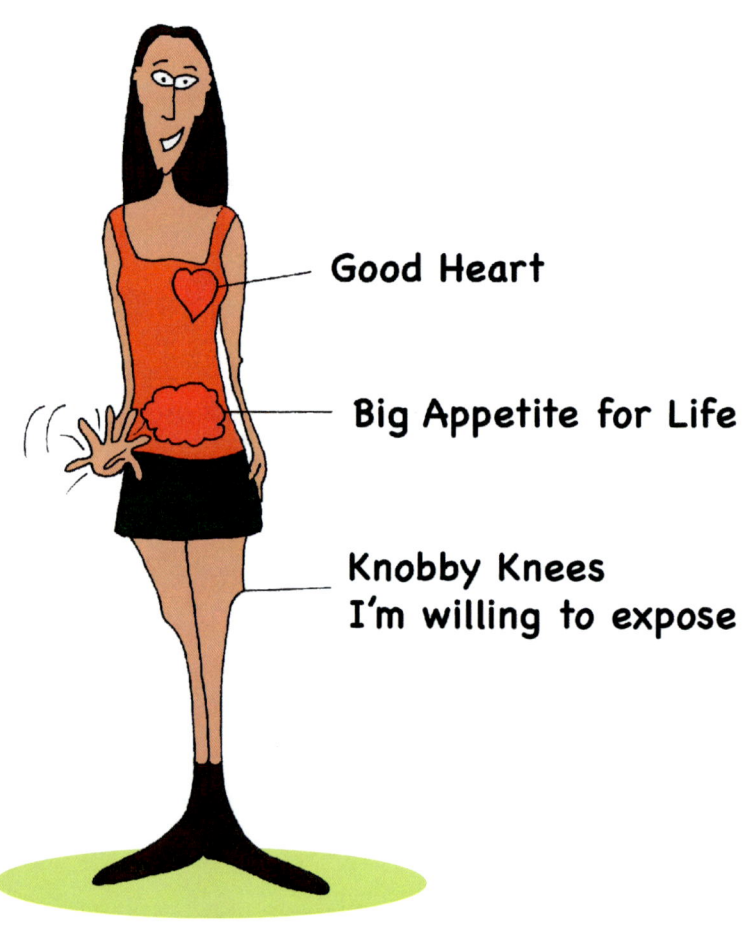

Good Heart

Big Appetite for Life

Knobby Knees
I'm willing to expose

# When I'm at the source, I'm **emotionally** calm and grounded...

# ...authentic and fearless...

# ...CREATIVE AND RESOURCEFUL.

## HALLOWEEN COSTUME PAINTED ON RECYCLED CARDBOARD

# I know my power
## and use it appropriately.

# But I don't take **myself** too seriously.

Whaen I'm at the source, I learn from anything, especially my mistakes. I'm always eager to share my *faux pas* with others so that they can learn too.

Guys, I have to apologize. Once again, I judged you because I wasn't invited to the last meeting. I realize now that I've felt left out for the last five years, but I never raised the issue. Please, accept my apology for my lack of pro-activity.

# Others are inspired to emulate me. When I'm at the source, I bring out the best in people.

I love being outside of my box! I feel authentic and free. And if I have negative emotions, that's okay, too, because when I'm at the source, I'm emotionally intelligent and self-accepting.

# Here I am now, trapped in my box. When I'm at the mercy, I'm a fallible human being too, but with far more fears and strategies to ward off perceived threats.

The tape: everything
I tend to repeat
when I'm in my box
(= mind chatter)

Protective
layers

Core
fears

# I know about being at the mercy very well. I've spent approximately

# 88%

# of my life in this state, thinking that my perceived threats were real.

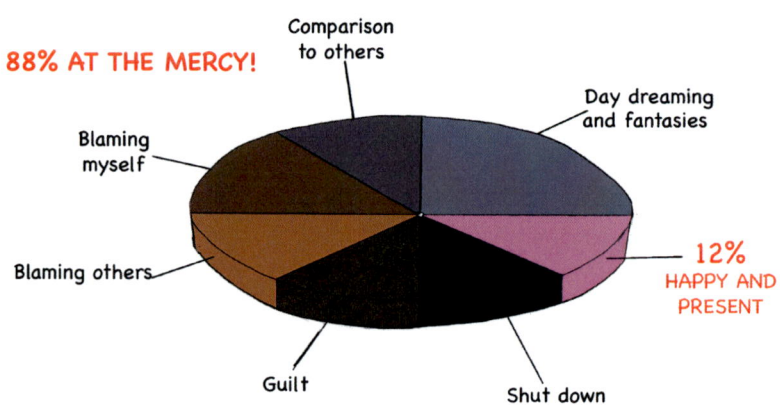

88% AT THE MERCY!

Comparison to others

Day dreaming and fantasies

Blaming myself

12% HAPPY AND PRESENT

Blaming others

Guilt

Shut down

The problem is that when I think inside of my box, my perception of reality is limited. My clarity tends to **shrink** while my misperceptions magnify.

1- PEOPLE don't listen to me...

2- THEY judge me and misunderstand me...

3- THEN THEY PLOT TO GET RID OF ME!!!

When I'm at the mercy, I worry about what others think of me. I have to prove that I'm an extraordinary human being, amazingly nice, incredibly insightful, completely competent, super-strong... oh, and hyper-humble! It's quite a spectacle.

# To perfect those images, I have to hide any hint of mediocrity, meanness, stupidity, self-centeredness or greed.
## It complicates my performance...

# ... and, it's exhausting.

# When I'm at the mercy,
## it's always someone else's fault.

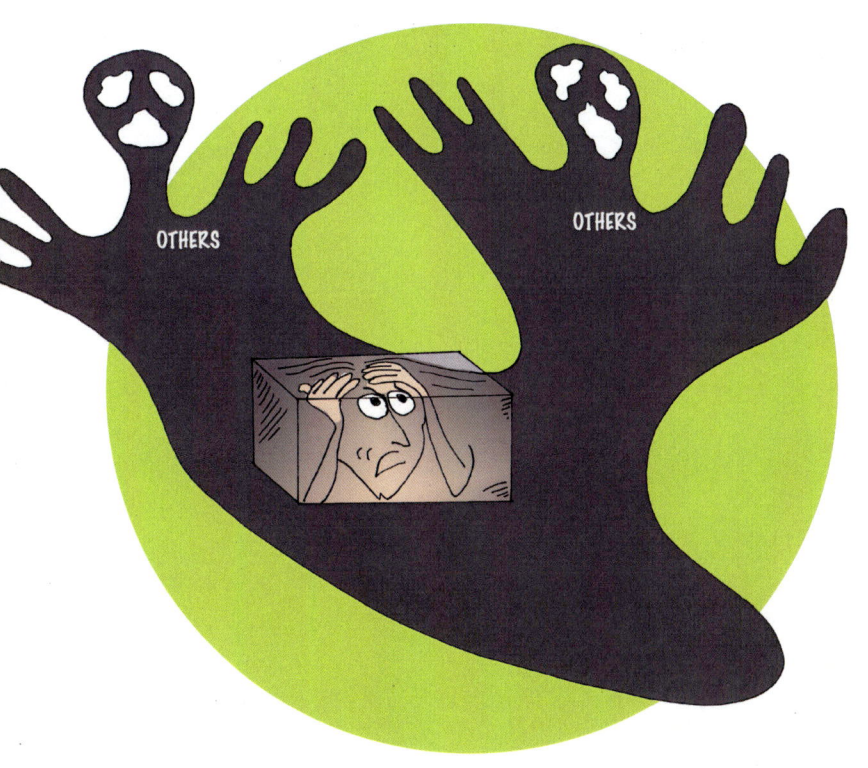

I judge my colleagues for being a bunch of fake, deluded people who are not speaking their truth and who ignore my exceptional value. I tend to ruminate over the same complaints, endlessly.

# Consequently,
## I create a self-fulfilling prophecy and everyone turns away from me.

But that's okay. Because even if I'm alone and miserable, at least, I'm RIGHT. And when I'm at the mercy, there is nothing more existentially meaningful than to be right.

I knew that my colleagues were a bunch of selfish, judgmental, fake, deluded people...

*Here is a tip if you don't know the difference between being at the mercy and being at the source: if you're sure that you are right, you are at the mercy.

# Unfortunately,
## when I bring my fears to the table, it has a domino effect.

Pretty soon, everyone becomes trapped in their boxes. That's when a team loses its inspirational vision, stamina, morale, and ability to co-create and have fun.

What a waste.

# chapter 3

# Hot Hot Hot Buttons

# If it feels so much better to be at the source, why aren't I always there? Because I have

# hot buttons.

As with others, my hot buttons cause me to react **ineffectively**, sometimes crazily, often in contradiction to everything I want.

**F**or a long time, I thought that I was reacting because *others* were **pushing** my buttons.

AN IRRATIONAL AND IRRESPONSIBLE STATEMENT:

Guys, you make me feel angry, confused and lost. My life is miserable because of you!

# But I've learned that only I am responsible for my emotional responses.

A rational woman who knows she's the one pushing her own buttons.

# When I'm triggered, it's because my brain detects a threat. Therefore, instead of having my pre-frontal cortex calmly handling the information and constructively resolving my issues...

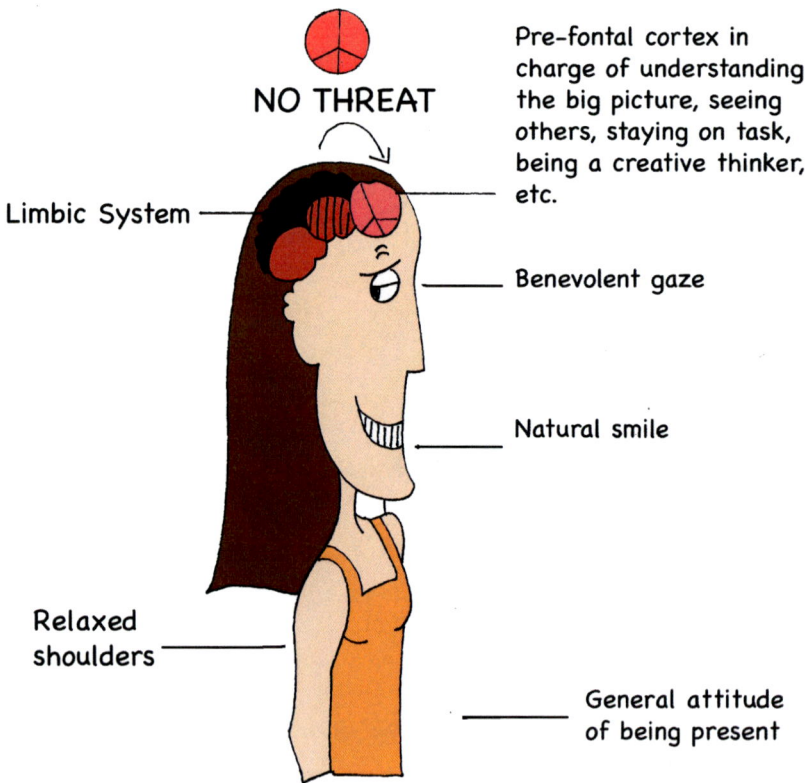

NO THREAT

Pre-fontal cortex in charge of understanding the big picture, seeing others, staying on task, being a creative thinker, etc.

Limbic System

Benevolent gaze

Natural smile

Relaxed shoulders

General attitude of being present

# ...my survival brain takes over with a fight or flight knee-jerk reaction...

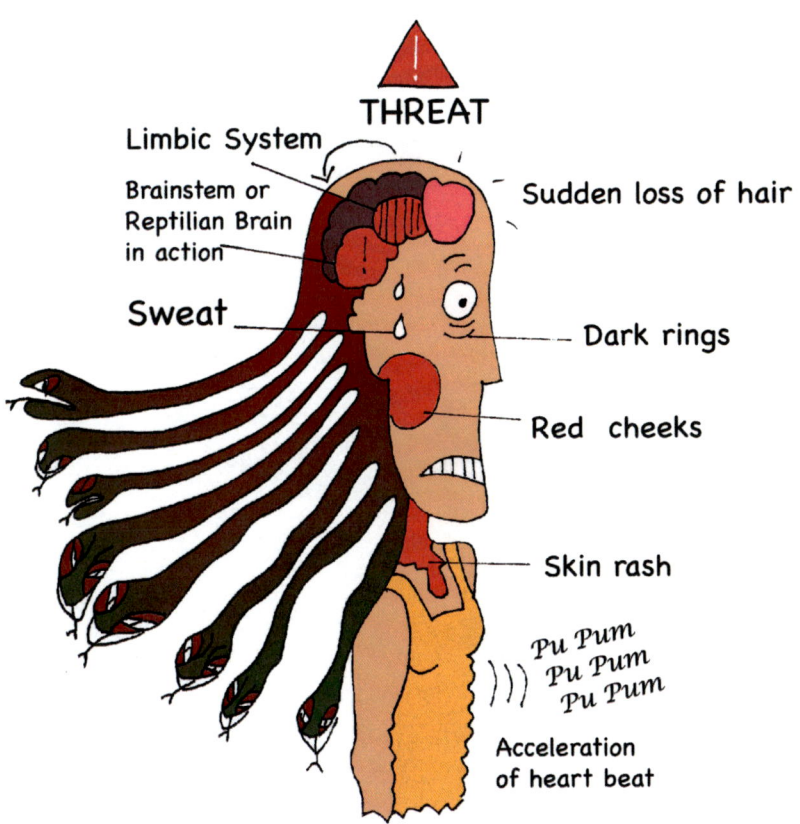

THREAT

Limbic System

Brainstem or Reptilian Brain in action

Sweat

Sudden loss of hair

Dark rings

Red cheeks

Skin rash

Pu Pum
Pu Pum
Pu Pum

Acceleration of heart beat

...a mechanism inherited
from our **ancestors** to cope
with real physical dangers.

(Flight
response)

# But today, at our office, those real physical dangers are rare.

# The problem is that the brain is often not good at differentiating real physical dangers from "perceived" threats.

**W**hen Andrea approached me about her project, I perceived a **threat** and switched to my box mode by adopting an arrogant-critical-judgmental attitude.

**B**eing **arrogant-critical-judgmental** is not who I  want to be. But, when I'm at the mercy, I'd rather appear DETESTABLE than...

Tight jaw
Monotone voice
Superior chin
Fixed composure

# ...LESS THAN...

# ...MY
# HOT HOT HOT
# BUTTON!

Why am I so reactive about feeling **"less than"** when my husband and all my friends aren't?

I don't care about being less than, as long as I'm not rejected.

# Until I joined my leadership company, I wasn't aware of this painful sensitivity.

True! It has only been a theme for the last twenty years!

# I drive **myself** nuts with my hot buttons, but over time, I've **discovered** that they are not all bad.

They are actually **useful** in identifying an underlying resistance I need to **explore** to step out of the box and return to my authentic self.

# It is my ego.

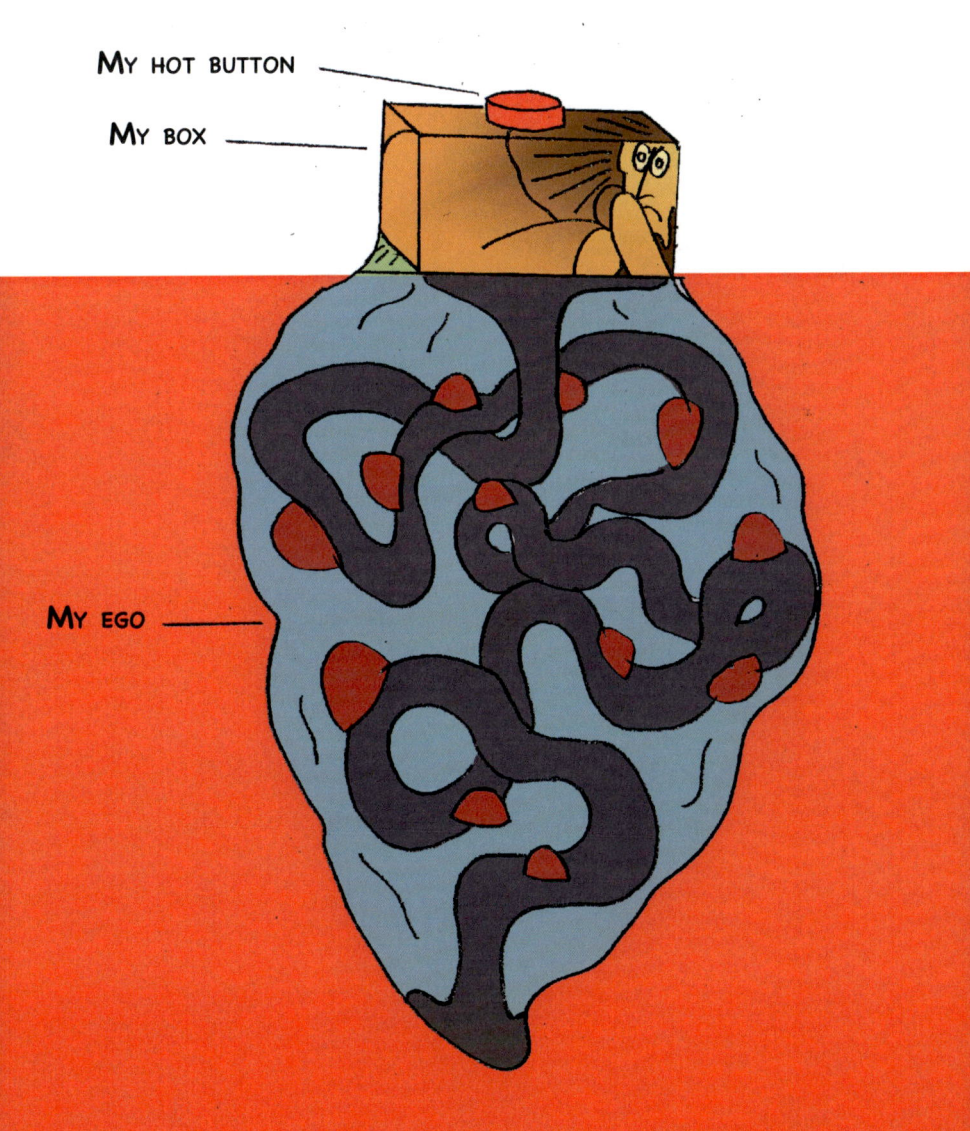

# chapter 4:

# The Candy Story

# No, I wasn't born in a box, feeling
# "less than."

**H**owever, I probably arrived on Earth, like most people, with a **combination** of genetic and familial influences.

In other **words**, with baggage.

Initially life was about sensations and gut feelings. Perhaps my heart was open and I felt unconditionally loved, but I don't remember. **Who does?**

# What I remember is the first time I went from feeling safe and joyful...

## ... to feeling confused and ashamed.

I t happened when I was five-years old, in a big supermarket in France in **1970**.

I am fascinated by the **magic** of the washing machines and study the details of their buttons.

I finally drag my eyes away and realize that my parents are gone.

I'm LOST!

# It's so terrifying that I don't remember anything after that moment...

...except being in the manager's office, where he calls my parents on the loudspeaker, and, in order to comfort me, gives me a candy.

## "Yea! I have a candy!"

T hat's probably what I said to my siblings when my family found me. **I wasn't bragging!** I was just happy to see them again. I thought they would be happy, too.

B ut, what I remember is that my siblings cried because I had a candy and they did not.

I was stupefied! Here I'd been abandoned and had a near-death experience, and all they cared about was candy?

**If, for my own family, I matter less than a candy, to whom will I matter?!**

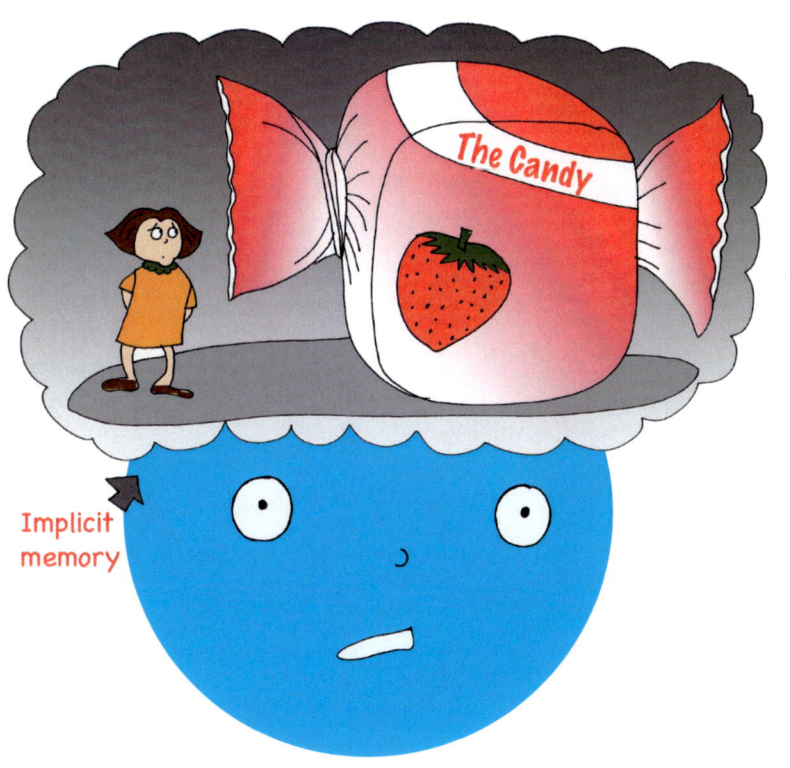

Implicit memory

To nobody? Am I worth less than a candy? Am I worthless? Is it bad to like candy? **What is wrong with me?**

**Thankfully, I forgot all these hideous doubts and went back to my life as a child.**

WORTH

EGOMETER

But *voilà!* My **ego** was born -the constant preoccupation with my self-worth.

# chapter 5

# The Ego-Clock

Mind you, I had a happy **childhood**. My parents were functional people, caring and resilient. My siblings were **playful** and **supportive**. In our home, there was an essential sense of **safety**.

**But, the candy event crystallized a series of fears and negative beliefs about me and the world, through which I started to process reality.**

By the time the candy episode passed, I had **become** my own alarm clock, waking up at six o'clock every morning, anxious about being late to preschool.

It never **crossed** my mind to ask my parents to wake me up.

I developed an **ego-filter** to protect myself: "Watch out! Others don't really care and are likely to disappoint you! So, you'd better take care of your needs yourself."

# At five, I was already
# OVERLY INDEPENDENT AND GUARDED!
# A first obstacle on the bumpy road to collaboration.

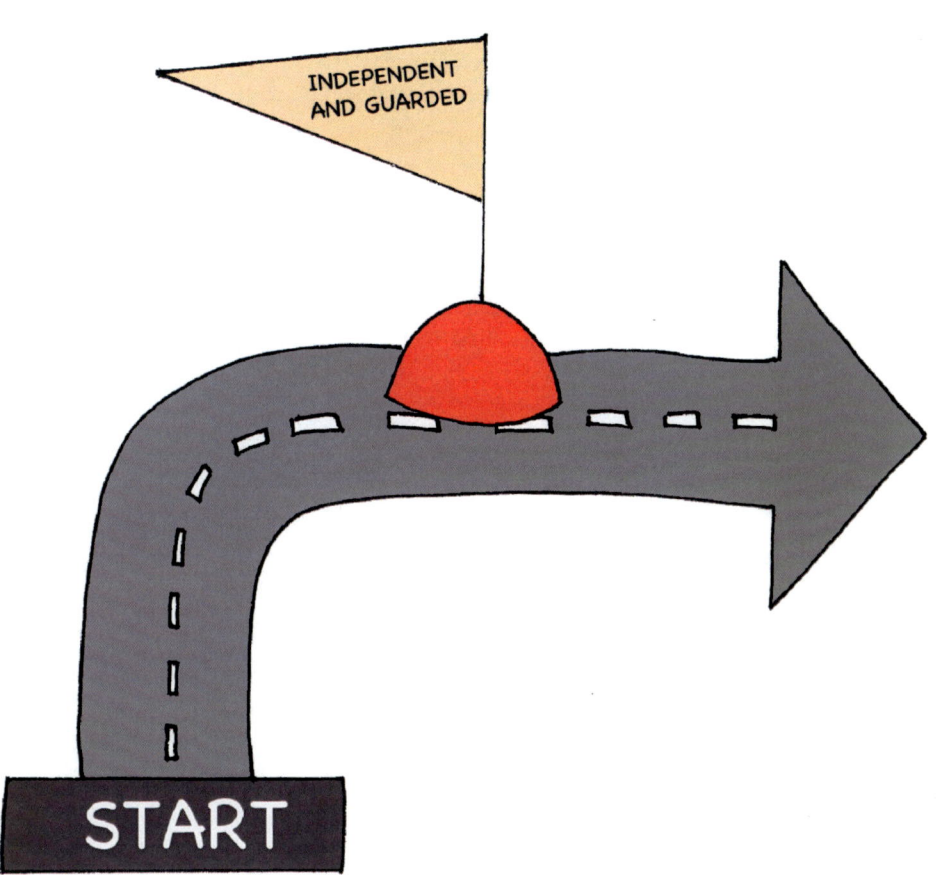

**A**t the same time, in my child's mind, arriving on time to preschool was proof of being as worthy as others : "Everyone else looks perfect and I'd better look perfect too." I had developed an **ego-driver** to prove my value.

**B**ut, I wasn't perfect. I had the hidden handicap of being worth less than a candy.

"Ego-flag"

PROVE YOUR WORTH!

# HIDING my flaws to appear STRONG AND PERFECT became another obstacle on the bumpy road to collaboration.

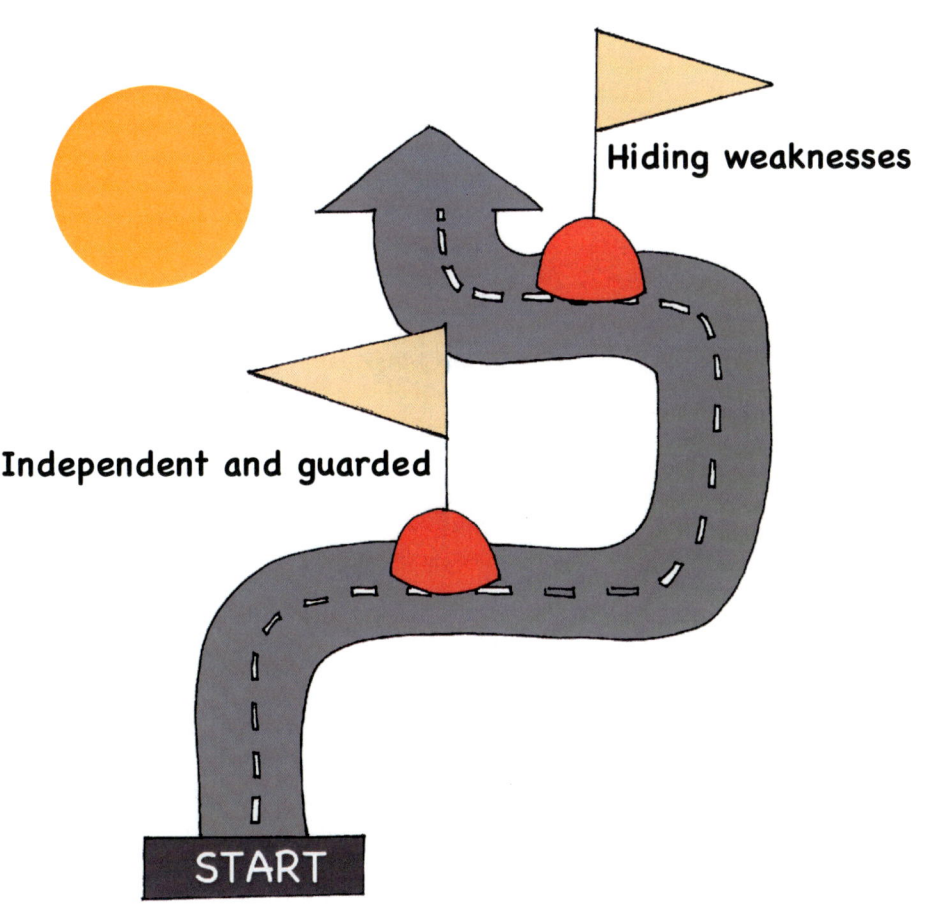

Hiding weaknesses

Independent and guarded

START

Expressing my emotions felt too **vulnerable. I feared I would be judged or, worse, ignored, if I let my feelings out. So, I learned to contain them. This was my first box.**

U nfortunately, the more I shut down my **feelings**, the less connected I was to myself, and the more I tried to prove my worth.

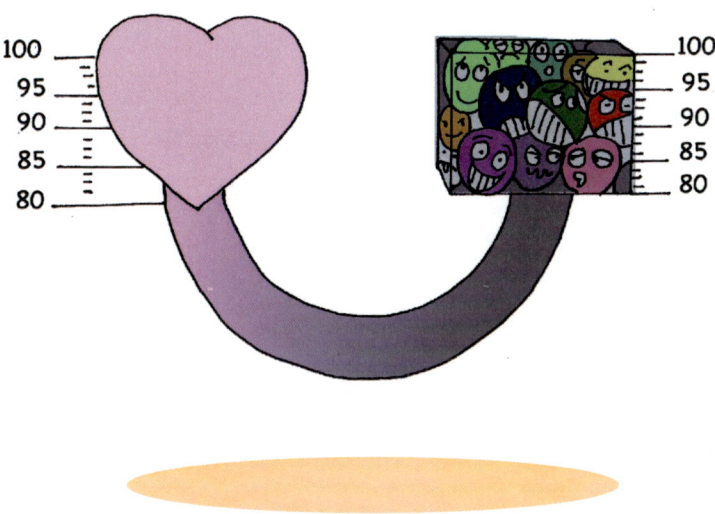

**E**ventually, simply being on time to school wasn't enough to reassure me of my **value**.

**W**ith my ego-driver in gear, I had to be SPECIAL and UNIQUE to avoid the danger of being **"less than."**

I have a great amount of value

Special and Unique

That's why, at seven-years old, I stopped playing the recorder when my older sister began. I could have learned music with her and we could have played together.

But, I had to be the ONLY ONE or not at all.

I have a great amount of value

Special and Unique

# When I let go of playing music with my sister, I threw myself into a second box.

F inding a **NICHE** where I would be the STAR became another obstacle on the bumpy road to you know what.

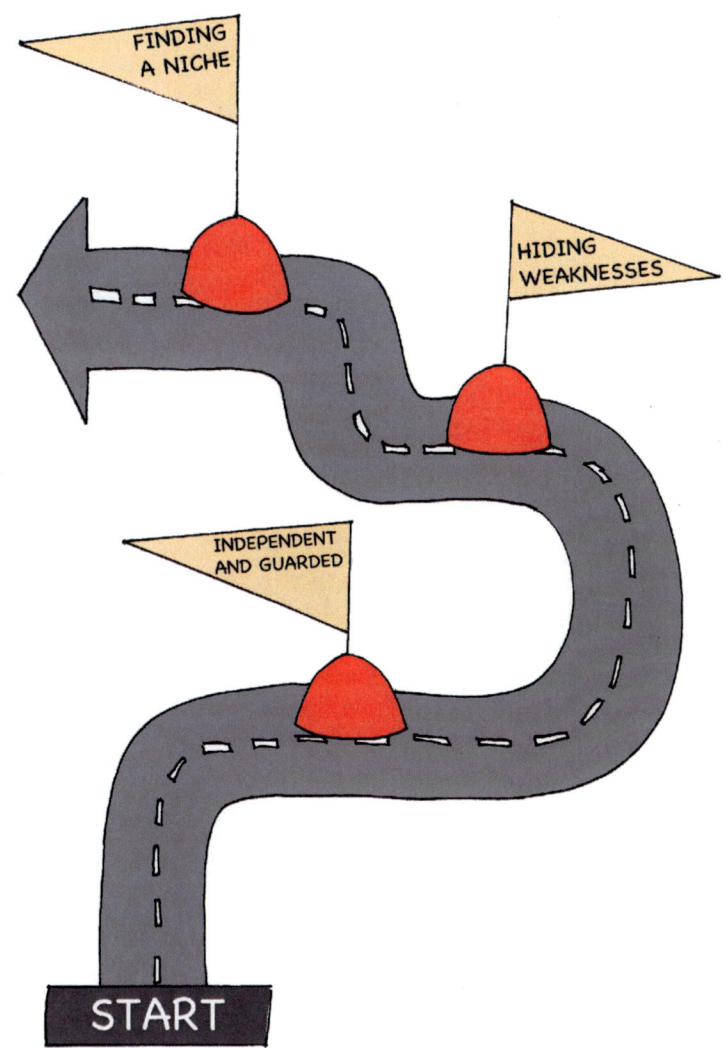

I could go on about the choices I've made to avoid appearing **"less than"** and proving I was special - all the opportunities lost, and all the obstacles built on the bumpy road to collaboration.

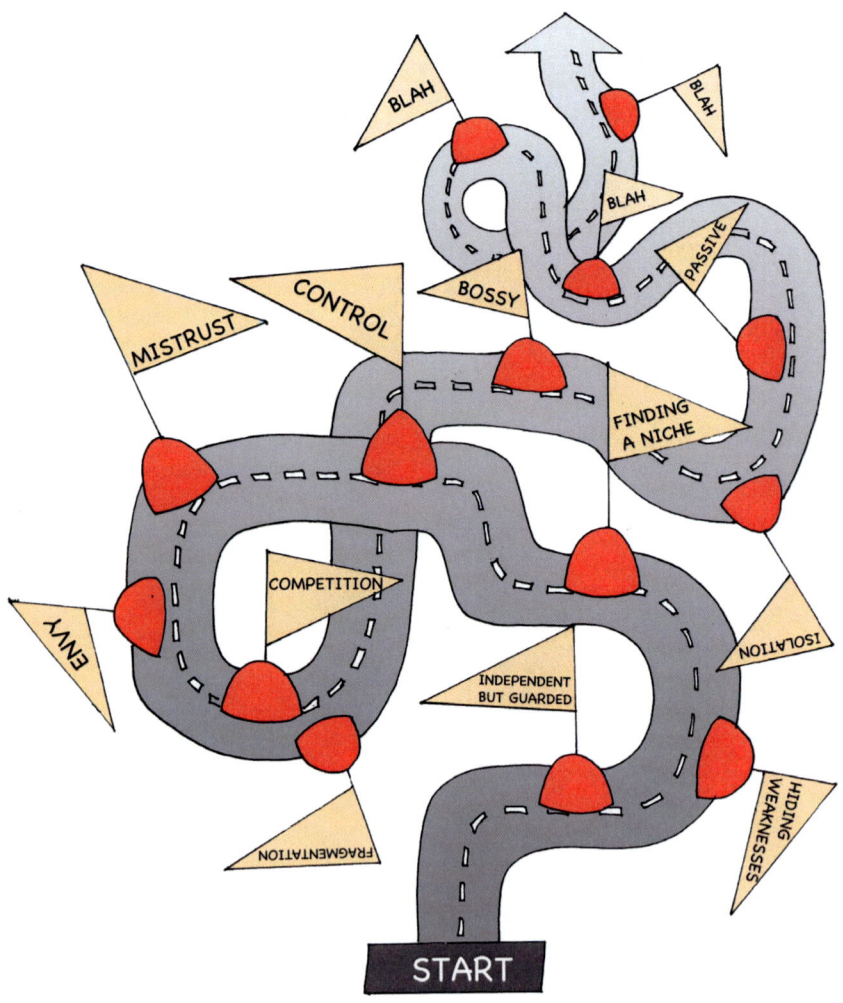

But, I won't. Eventually, the constraints of being in my box became intolerable. I was fossilized. At 25, I realized that I had no choice but to break free.

Today, after many years of soul searching and personal exploration, my hot buttons humbly remind me that I still have ego wounds to heal.

But, when I'm triggered and fall into my box, I can sometimes step out of it in a nano-second!

# chapter 6

# Twelve Steps Toward Freedom

Let's return to the reality that three days after my inauthentic interaction with Andrea, I'm still in my box. My territory seems safe and has the appearance of collaboration. I am momentarily relieved, with just a shadow of guilt. It's not great, but it's not terrible either.

My instinct tells me that I could do better. **Thankfully**, I've developped a series of twelve practical steps to clarify my choices. Sometimes I need to follow all of the steps. Other times I need just one. There is no quick fix to step out of a box, but there are a lot of possibilities!

STEPS

TOOLBOX

# 1

# PRACTICE SELF-AWARENESS

First step, I look at myself and ask, Am I the authentic person I want to be? Would I be my best friend?

# CHOOSE A PATH

**At the mercy**  **At the source**

This way is the same old way. You end up where you started...

This way...

... more bitter.

... who knows! The hero's journey!

I f the answer is no, I need to make a choice.

# CLARIFY WHAT I DON'T WANT

Choosing to stay in my box is an option. However, if I want to be at the source and I'm too stuck to move, at least I can clarify what I don't want.

For example, I imagine what happens if I avoid Andrea because of my shame:

To justify my avoidance, I criticize her, first through passive-aggressive comments, then openly. My colleagues notice that I've created a bad atmosphere, but I'm too trapped in my box to let go. Now, I blame all my colleagues who have become tired of me. I'm eventually fired. I have to numb my resentment with anger, righteousness and cigarettes. I release my emotions onto my husband who divorces me. I become a vagrant in the street and I destroy my life.

Facing this projection of negative consequences brings an emotional light to what I need to do.

But, I may be overwhelmed with guilt and still paralyzed.

# 4

# EMPATHY FOR MYSELF

By refusing to succumb to guilt and accepting my fallible nature, I can access empathy for myself.

# 5

# IDENTIFY MY HOT BUTTON

Being guilt-free doesn't guarantee being box-free, but it liberates brain space. Now I have more energy to grab a pen and a piece of paper and investigate my hot button.

| *Facts* | *Thoughts* |
|---|---|
| I meet my colleague at the coffee machine. She announced me that she's going to create a sustainable departement in our company. Her clients will include our non-profit organizations. | Who is she to create something I already created?! Now she arrives with her big MBA plan to use MY work to create "Our" department?!! She'll be MY boss and I'll have to report to her?!!! She's unrealistic, she wants to take over, she wants to steal my place. She's insensitive to others work. It's not the first time I notice this tendency ... Boy, how pathetic I am to have such thoughts. It's sad to be territorial at my age. It's uncool to be judgmental. I have to hide my thoughts but make su she's not going to create a department that threatens my position in the company. At the same time, I want to show ~~her~~ that I am still collaborative. At least I'm taking her into account. I can't believe that she didn't kn I was the one in charge. What a lack of respect. She's so self We always have to fight for our position in our company. If I don't bragg, nobody will notice my job. |

A little bit of journaling to sort the facts
from the mindchatter...

... and no surprise. It's the same old sweet spot. In my interaction with Andrea, I felt like I was less than a candy.

# 6

# DEVELOP A SENSE OF HUMOR

Rediscovering my candy fixation allows me to laugh. Having a sense of humor can be transformative.

# 7

# EMPATHY FOR OTHERS

However, if I can't access my sense of humor because I'm so preoccupied with myself, the only way out is to have empathy for others...

These shoes look worn but they are warm, solid and reliable. They brought Andrea to Seattle every month during two years of working on her MBA... No wonder Andrea didn't know exactly what my responsibilities were  at the office... She wasn't there.

...put myself in Andrea's shoes.

# REHEARSE A DIFFICULT CONVERSATION

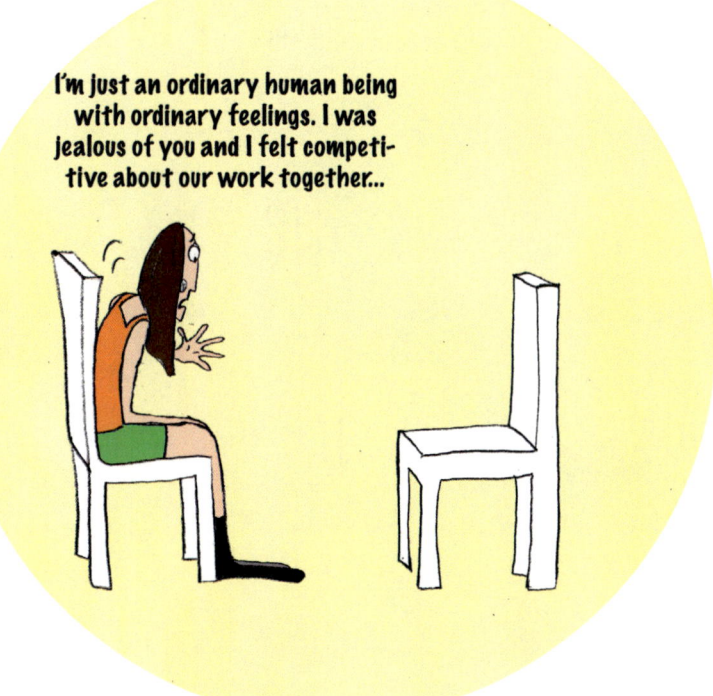

S tanding in Andrea's shoes helps me to connect to her heart. I'm ready to make a move and have a vulnerable conversation. First, I rehearse what I want to say.

But, what if she's too busy to listen
to me? What if she's arrogant?
Condescending? What if she laughs at me?

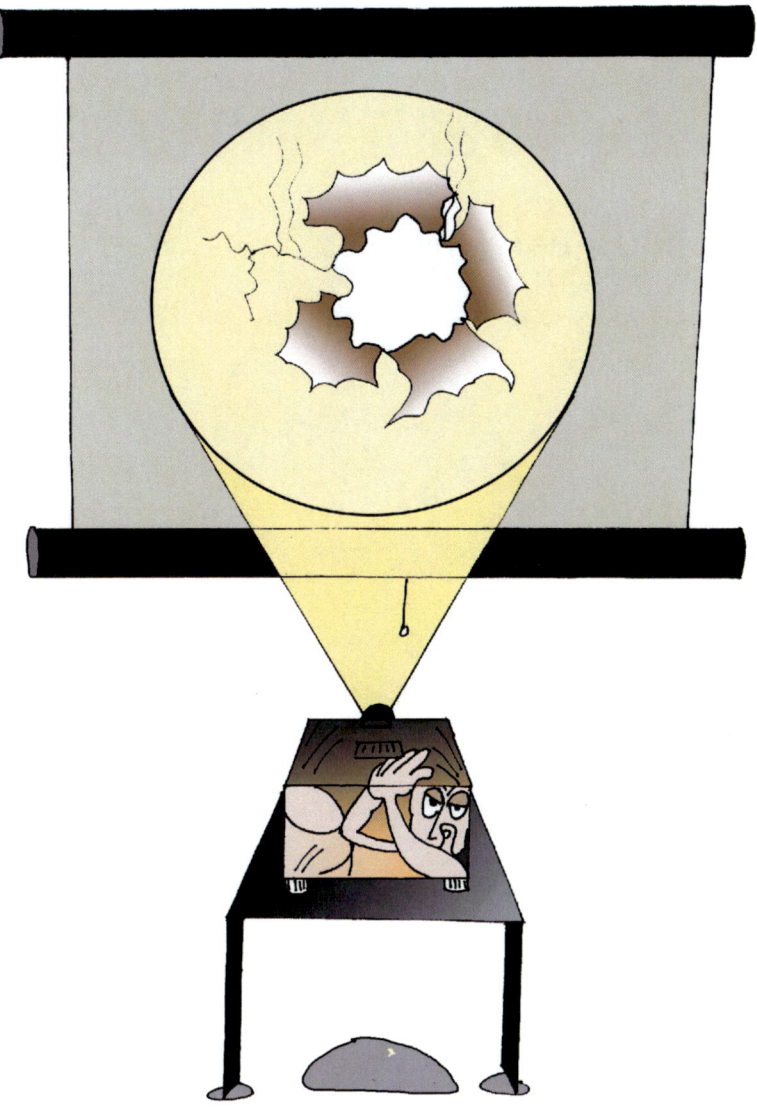

Gulp. I prefer to retract into box
mode rather than risk being shamed.

# SAY "SO WHAT" TO MY FEARS

SO WHAT if you're
LESS THAN A
CANDY?!!!

A setback invites me to apply a radical step: the "So what?" principle. So what if she overlooked me and acted as if she was more important than me?

# RECONNECT WITH MY ASPIRATIONS AND GOALS

More important than any of my ego-fears is my desire to focus on my higher aspirations and essential life goals. Like most people, I strive to do meaningful and impactful work.

If I care about the environnment and leaving a sustainable earth to the next generation (especially my daughter and my possible future grandchildren and great grandchildren and the whole tribe that will possibly succeed my little "me" and my little husband)...

If I care about birds, bees and pollination, bio-diversity, forests, polar bears, tasty and diverse vegetables, metal-free water in my glass and healthy fish in the sea... In short, if I care about the natural beauty of Mother Earth...

# DO I REALLY WANT TO POISON THE ATMOSPHERE WITH MY TOXIC THOUGHTS AND FALSE SMILE?

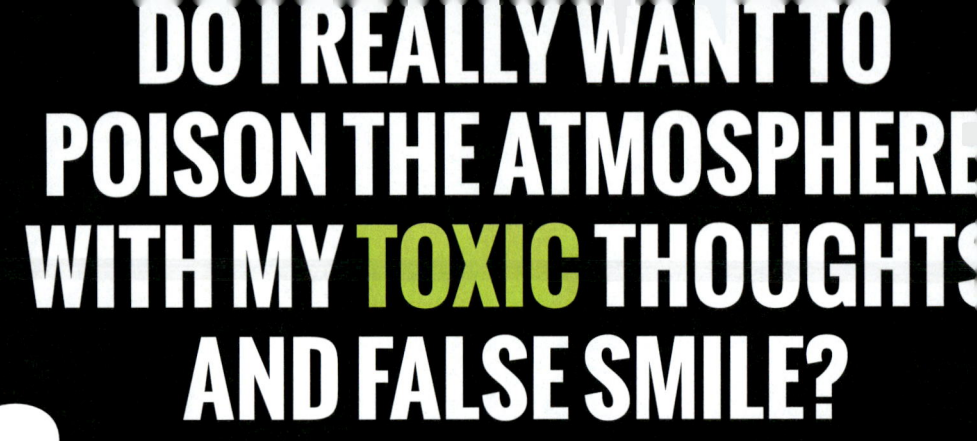

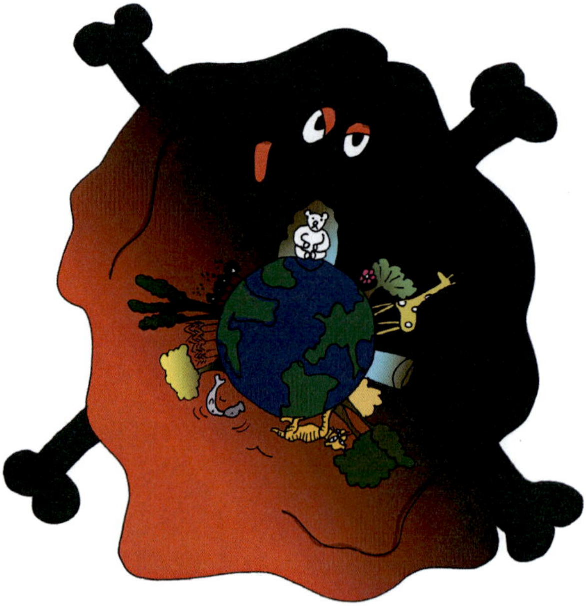

Absolutly not. I want to create a playful and collaborative environment for me and my colleagues, and have the energy to write great books. **I want to be free.**

But, sometimes my hottest buttons won't let me be free, even though it feels like I've tried everything.

Acquiring freedom can be dependent on a quality that we post-modern-industrialized people tend to forget.

# 11

# TRUST THE PASSAGE OF TIME

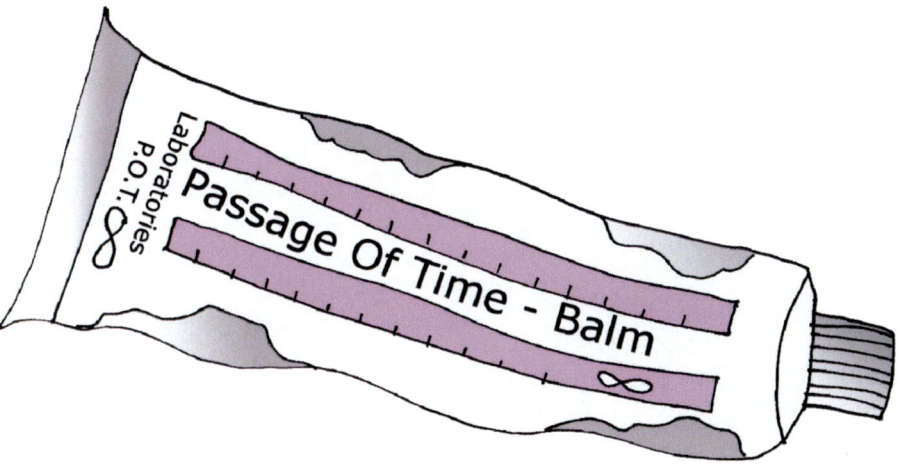

The Passage of Time (P.O.T.) is a balm for the ego-blow and helps diminish the intensity of the original trigger.

The P.O.T. also provides space to practice recentering activities that typically help to open the heart and cool down the hot button. For example:

At this point, if I'm still in my box, I might start to panic and have a crisis of self-doubt. Is my heart that closed ? What's wrong with me?

Nothing. I just need to take a leap of faith and ask for help.

## 12
# ASK FOR HELP

I can ask for help from the universe! I'm not alone! I can also ask for help from my spouse, friends, children, colleagues, neighbors, coaches, parents, in-laws and goldfish...

...so that my heart can expand. Now empathy can caress me as gently as a feather. I can open to the goodness in humanity. And the noisy excruciating "BLAH, BLAH, BLAH" of my mental process can finally shut up.

Congratulations to me! I'm out of my box, ready to expose myself and have a real conversation with Andrea.

## chapter 7

# The Resolution: When Colleagues Reconnect

# I went to see Andrea. With no expectations, I shared all my vulnerable feelings. She was surprised, but not horrified.

S he actually **apologized**. She had been so anxious to create a school project and maintain her identity at work that she failed to acknowledge the work I had done already. Clearly, expressing my vulnerability allowed Andrea to do the same.

# H
**H**er earnestness made me feel **understood** and connected. I apologized too.

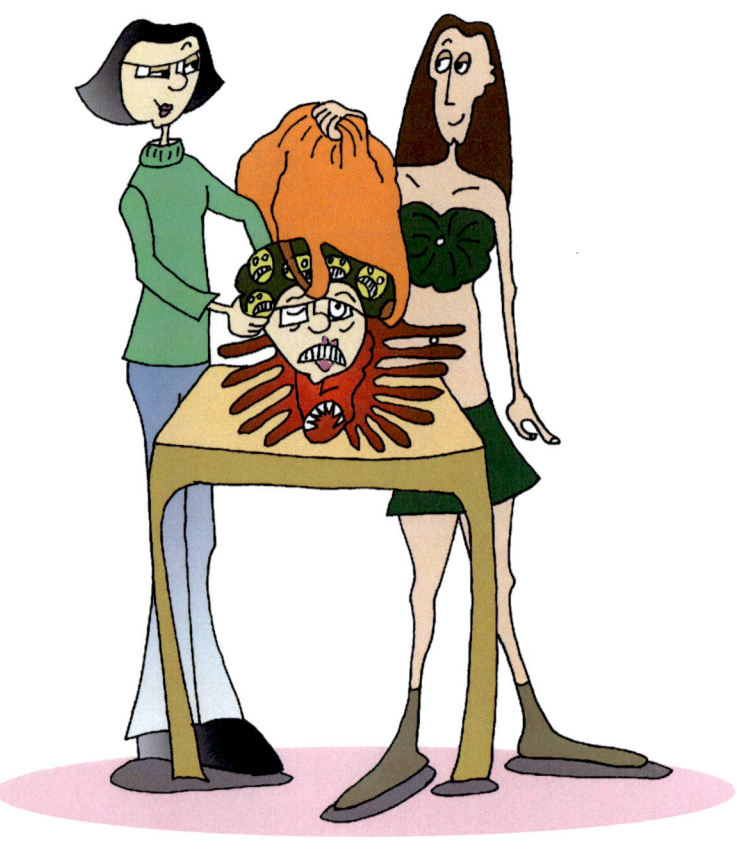

# She felt safe enough to confess her difficulty in asking for help.

# I smiled and conceded that I have the same issue.

Together, we were able to wash our "dirty laundry." By acknowledging our fears and by **understanding** where the other one stood, we stopped the cycle of judgments.

# W

e realigned our higher purpose: **creating** a **sustainable** organization by changing our competitive culture, starting with supporting each other. It felt great.

And when she suggested that I should be the boss of the combined sustainability and non-profit department, it felt TERRIFIC.

**B**ut, I realized that **I didn't need to be the boss anymore.** At this point, my heart was open and I was 100% ready to collaborate with my colleague...

# ... with my team...

# ...and with my extended community!

THE END

# Ac-knowl-edg-ments

T hanks to the LAL team for their ongoing support and friendship. Thanks to the co-founders of the original methodology: Claire Nuer, who mentored me for many years and invited me to draw when I had forgotten my passion; Sami Cohen, for his enthusiasm and affection. Thanks to Noah Nuer, who held my hand when I was trying to find my artistic path. Thanks to Shayne Hughes, Lara Nuer, Nathalie Salles, Marc-André Olivier, Jean-Pierre Guilhaume, Laura Gates, Fila-ree Radich, Samantha Cooprider and Céline Meunier, for being my lifelong friends and colleagues. I moved from France to the United States to work with them. Thanks to Elizabeth Freuler, Leeann Mallorie, Ariel Goodman, Jonathan London, Tamara Trussell, Charlene Wilson, and Amy Logan, the new generation that inspires me with fresh ideas. Thanks to all my buddies in France who participated in creating the LAL journey.

Thanks to Susan Isa Efros, friend, author and writing coach without whom this book wouldn't exist AT ALL. Not only has Susan helped me to write in grammatically correct English, but her humor, wisdom and creativity invaluably enriched my own vision. She has supported me in finding my artistic voice and believing in myself. This has been an amazing collaboration!

Thanks to all the other readers of this project who provided advice and encouragement: Aimée Lyndon-Adams, Allison Fragakis, Amy Logan, Aurélie Blard-Quintard, Carol Ross, Emily Fishman, Jean-Pierre Guilhaume, Judy Bornstein, Lara Nuer, Karen Leland, Laura Gates, Marc-André Olivier, Michel Abitteboul, Monique Gauthier, Nathalie Salles, Noah Nuer, Robin Ely, Shayne Hughes, Tamara Trussell, Gilles Lévy and Thierry Ramière.

Thanks to my clients for their trust over the eleven years I've worked in the United States. They welcomed me, despite my strong French accent and cultural naiveté. Our collaboration has been a source of endless pleasure.

A heartfelt thanks to my husband (and colleague) Jean-Pierre and my daughter, Anouk. They are both truly more important than my books, but they give me the space to make my books as important as them. They are my anchors.

Finally, I'm grateful to my parents, Albert and Monique, and siblings, Myriam, Gilles and Alexandra who always supported my life choices with care and respect, especially when they were outside of the box!

# Glossary

**The tape: Everthing I say and think in the box.**

**AT THE MERCY/IN THE BOX:** I use the terms "at the mercy" and "in the box" interchangeably. At Learning as Leadership (LAL), "at the mercy" is a deluded state of confusion driven by fear. We have limited perception of reality and don't see all our options.

Note: I use the expression "being in the box" because it's a visual representation of this constricted state. Thanks again to the Arbinger Institute, which has allowed me to use their copyrighted concepts of "being in the box" and "being outside of the box."

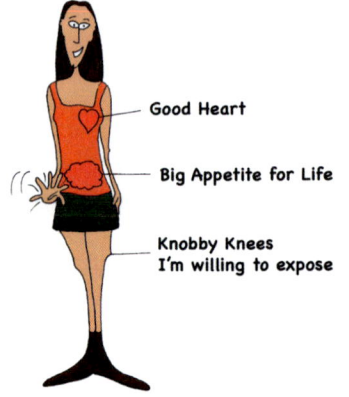

Good Heart

Big Appetite for Life

Knobby Knees
I'm willing to expose

**AT THE SOURCE/OUTSIDE OF THE BOX:** At LAL we speak about being "at the source," a state of clarity where we are authentic, present, engaged and connected to others. When we are at the source, we act from a centered place and have full access to our intuition and natural wisdom.

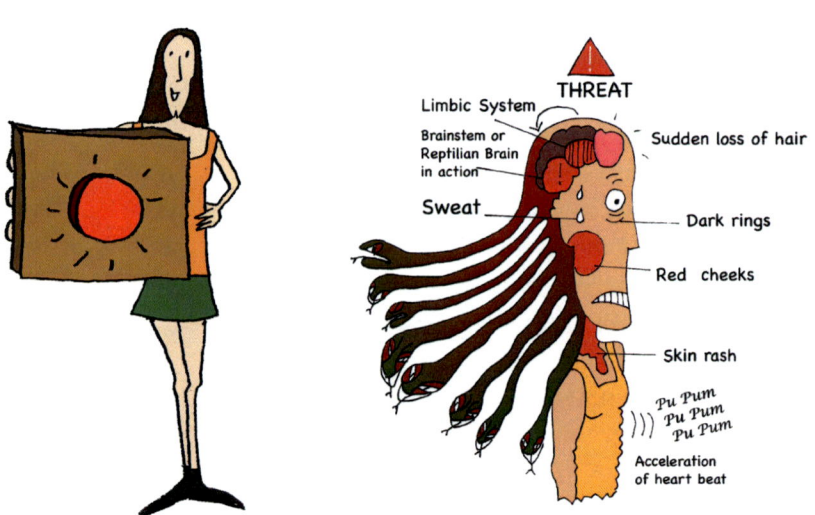

THREAT

Limbic System

Brainstem or
Reptilian Brain
in action

Sweat

Sudden loss of hair

Dark rings

Red cheeks

Skin rash

Pu Pum
Pu Pum
Pu Pum

Acceleration
of heart beat

**HOT BUTTON:** A point of sensitivity that the ego recognizes as a threat. When a hot button is triggered, our perception of reality is limited and distorted. We react ineffectively with fight or flight responses.

**THE EGO:** The constant preoccupation with one's self-worth. At LAL, we speak about EGO-SYSTEMS™, the ensemble of automatic strategies driven by the urge to protect or inflate the self-image.

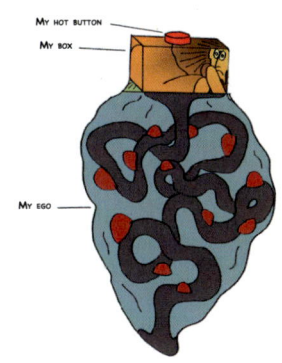

**THE TWELVE STEPS TOWARD FREEDOM:** Adapting LAL tools and concepts, I've created my own twelve steps of how to break free from the ego's constraints.

**1 - PRACTICE SELF-AWARENESS:** Be conscious of our thoughts, behaviors, and emotions in order to act according to our authentic values.

**2 - CHOOSE A PATH:** There is no neutral state: we are either at the mercy or at the source. If we don't actively choose, we stay in our habitual counter-productive reactions.

**3 - CLARIFY WHAT WE DON'T WANT:** It is often easier to clarify what we want, if first we clarify what we don't want.

**4 - EMPATHY FOR THE SELF:** Accept our fallible nature and care for the self, instead of being self-critical or over-indulging in guilt.

**- IDENTIFY HOT BUTTONS:** Investigate our hot buttons/ego-threat. Search for the emotional resemblance between a current and a past trigger. Naming the hot button makes explicit the negative emotion, and its release possible.

**6 - DEVELOP A SENSE OF HUMOR:** If we can laugh at our hot buttons, bravo! It's proof of personal mastery, and that the trigger has been de-activated.

**- EMPATHY FOR OTHERS:** This is as important as empathy for ourselves. It helps us to expand our perception and develop compassion.

## 8 - REHEARSE A DIFFICULT CONVERSATION

Practice being honest and vulnerable. This can lead to a more effective encounter because while preparing, we can make further discoveries to master our hot buttons.

## 9 - SAY, SO WHAT? TO OUR FEARS:
The most difficult transformative step is to look at our worst fears and accept that they could come true. Once we accept our fears, the magic of the present moment can unfold. We can focus on what's essential. This concept was developed by Claire Nuer when she was facing terminal cancer.

## 10 - RECONNECT WITH OUR ASPIRATIONS AND GOALS:
They help us transcend our ego. At LAL, we search for a central intention, or a NOBLE GOAL, that monitors our entire life.

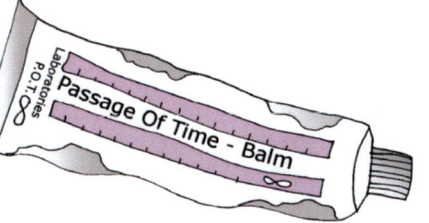

## 11 - TRUST THE PASSAGE OF TIME:

When we surrender to the passage of time, our hot buttons cool down. It's about letting go and appropriately using our time to practice recentering activities.

## 12 - ASK FOR HELP: Asking for help is the most vulnerable commitment to transformation. When we reach out, the universe becomes generous.

# To learn more about my work, visit my website:

www.carole-levy.com

# Hot Button Journal

# Hot Button Journal

## 1.-Triggering event

Ex: Andrea announced her new idea: she's going to create a Sustainability Department that will include our non-profit clients.

## 2.-Internal thoughts

She's unrealistic, she wants to steal my place, she wants to take over...

## 3.-Resulting emotions

Resentful, protective, frustrated.

# Hot Button Journal

**4.-Underlying hot button**

I'll be less than a candy.

**5.-Which of the 12 steps are helpful?**

In my case, I needed all of them!